To Derek 10-9-19
Don

D1250119

ISBN 978-1-7336103-2-2 (print)
978-1-7336103-3-9 (eBook)

Published by Arjuna Books
600 3rd Avenue, 42nd Floor
New York, NY 10016

* This book is a revised edition originally published under the pseudonym of Max McBride.

TENEBRAE:
A Memoir of Love and Death

Dan Flanigan

2019

CONTENTS

FOREWORD

Dan Flanigan is a visionary poet. His series of poems, *Tenebrae: A Memoir of Love and Death,* based on an ancient service sometimes performed in the Roman Catholic Church, grapples with the death of his wife. In these poems he takes the reader on the journey that his wife endured, and he with her, in her wrenching passage from life to death. I initially read his manuscript some time ago but still I am filled with its humanity, its depth of vision, and imagination. One of the things that resonates with me most is how willing he was to explore the *hardest stuff* in order to find his voice. He found it. These poems are some of the most moving poems I have ever read about death. What he has created is astonishing. There is a humanity at the core of these pieces that shakes the reader to the bone. They are moving. They are elegiac. They are celebratory. If sadness and solitude make for big art, these poems are big art. But they are more than that—they are the human heart in a singular and authentic voice. Flanigan's poetry is everything that I think of when I think of what poetry should be—playful, intelligent, of the personal and the universal simultaneously. So, while the poems have a confessional air to them, they are completely of us, for us, the world at large.

Other of the poems in this book focus on family, on history, on his Irish heritage. In particular, there is a piece entitled "San Josef Bay, Cape Scott, Vancouver Island," which recounts a walk and conversation between a father and his young daughter. The writing in the prose poem is magical, haunting, and utterly sublime because of what Dan says and does not say all at once. He has that ability, that talent, to know what not to say, to impose silence into a piece, the unsaid, in order to say more, in order to garner the most powerful emotional effect possible.

This is Dan Flanigan's power—his poetry is an emotional poetry. It is not a sentimental poetry, though. It gets at the heart of the heart and tears things up to build them back up. It is a smart poetry. The ethos of his voice is strong. When you read his work, you feel like you are in the hands of a master craftsperson, in the hands of a poet who has figured out the big and gorgeous balance between 'here and there' at the same time. Like the Tenebrae poems, his other pieces, though different in subject matter, come from the same well-spring and express, again, the depth of humanity that is so heartbreaking and exquisite in his work.

Dan Flanigan's poems are for the world, for every man and woman who wants to know more about the beauty and the suffering that are in a state of constant collision.

—Matthew Lippman

Author of A Little Gut Magic, The New Year of Yellow, Monkey Bars, Salami Jew, and *American Chew*

TENEBRAE

TENEBRAE

INTRODUCTION

The Tenebrae ("shadows" or "darkness" in Latin) is an ancient service sometimes performed in the Roman Catholic Church and certain other Christian denominations during Holy Week (also called Passion Week). Many composers—Palestrina, Tallis, Gesualdo, and, more recently, Golijov—have set the Tenebrae to music.

The central feature of the Tenebrae is the gradual extinguishment of candles, fifteen of them, accompanied by readings of psalms and other sacred texts, the extinguishment of the last candle plunging the church into total darkness. The ceremony terminates in a movement called the Strepitus (meaning "Great Noise" and symbolizing the earthquake that followed Christ's death), whereupon the congregation leaves the church in silence.

Although my Tenebrae is not religious in any traditional sense, the structure, mood, and dramatic progression of this ancient ritual seemed to perfectly suit my mournful purpose.

1

SONORA

The desert crunched beneath our booted feet.
Lone figures in a landscape,
Atop the first foothill we stopped to rest.
Below us the valley we had come through,
Above us the farther hills,
Above them the jagged treeless mountain,
Above that Jove's cauldron,
Where light and dust
Birth sunsets of crimson fire,
Lemon-streaked, marbled blue, black-roofed,
Colors of another spectrum,
Yes, made by Something Like God.
You wore a snow-white t-shirt,
Tan shorts and legs and arms and neck and face,
Your hair cut short in a boyish bob.
I wanted you then, I still so do
But never, never, never, never now.

It was a desert,
Yet we marveled how green it was,
Barrel cacti spiked like maces,
Palo verde trees, gnarled and skeletal but rooted deep,
Yucca, creosote, mesquite, ocotillo,
Swaths of yellow poppies,
A Golgotha of saguaros
Lined like crucifixes on a Roman highway,
Sprouting blood-red flowers,
Jumping cholla with spikes that seize you,
Trap you faster and faster as you struggle to escape,

They will not free you unless you cut them away.
Gila woodpeckers and Gila monsters.
Rattlesnakes, scorpions, tarantulas.
So many birds all around us,
Twittering and racketing in the underbrush.
Quail skittering in mincing steps.
Roadrunners like wicked witches arrogantly prancing.
Did we fall into a quarrel that day
As we so often carelessly did?
We were so young then
We thought we had love to squander,
And time too since we would surely never die.
I think now that we failed to notice
The jackrabbits tall and gaunt and trembling,
Their unblinking hysterical eyes,
The hawks gliding on thermal waves,
The darting lizards that could not stay hidden,
Scooting along in a zigzagging waddle,
Stopping every few yards and glancing sharply to the sky,
From which Death swoops down and strikes low.
We did not know then what we do know now——
You are, you become, then are no more.

2

QUILLS

I see you both far from me and near.
Barely more than children when we met,
First semester freshmen,
A drunken evening in our college town,
Two deluded porcupines,
Hoping our quills were feathers.

So it began, love's desperate battle,
You of the imperious will,
"Sheriff" as I took to calling you,
The girl who tossed
Your old boyfriend's cloddish wing-tipped shoes
Right out the car window.

I, a beast with no trust or clue
Why one so beautiful
Would bother with one such as me.
Chestnut eyes in Modigliani face,
Bare legs in miniskirt,
Auburn hair flowing down your back,
False eyelashes and nails,

Big dark circles of mascara.
Your parvenu parents,
Stood fast against me, us, you
For years and years,
Disapproving of a mongrel from Rust Town.
I even wore then an ugly many-colored winter coat
Just like a matted-fur mutt would sport.

My judgment was probably the "grave injustice" you said it was,
("You do me a grave injustice," you said,
As if we were characters in a Victorian novel.)
But then you didn't exactly help, telling me early on
How you intended to marry a rich old man.
And I was not wise enough then to understand
That was just some inevitable residue,
An involuntary twitch of sorts
From living all your life under that roof.
I should have understood and forgiven it at once,
Seen that you had a rebel's heart.
But instead it fed my mistrust of you,
A suspected fifth columnist from the evil kingdom.
If it is a rich man you want, then why me?
Poor and determined to stay poor,
And above all unhappy, desperately, willfully unhappy
Because surely all sensitive souls must be so.

You were the enemy of my quest, I thought,
And you never actually denied that,
Yet years later you said it was my "dreams" that captured you.
Why did it take you so long to say so?
Because until then it was not safe to do?
Hedging your bet,
Afraid to plunge with me over the side,
Leaving the last strip of dry land behind,
Yet you did go over with me time after time.
Splash!
But always clutching in your trailing hand
A life-vest.

With serious mien and furrowed brow
We plotted our consummation,
In those scary times of "getting knocked up"
And "having to get married."

Bumbling pioneers of the sexual revolution
(Well, more like homesteaders really).
If you said the right words to the local public health people
They would hand you the keys to freedom's door,
Birth control pills!
Weeks of appointments to secure those,
Wait another 28 days for them to "take,"
Then a blanket in the woods,
Gnats buzzing overhead,
Both of us disgusted,
Mere foreplay was so much better than this,
Too much plan and too little passion,
The first time is the worst time,
But there was never another bad time,
Except our wedding night of course.

From beginning to end,
It was porcupine love,
Quills flying.
Many times I said
That if we talked long enough about anything
Hostilities would ensue.
No immediate causes for these wars,
Now, racking my brain, I can't remember even one,
Because, I guess, the cause was always remote—
Never fully reconciled to our differences
And mistrusting something
Traitorous that we thought we sensed
Deep within each other's core.

Now that you're gone
I want to think it was mostly I who was at fault,
But surely that lets you off the hook too easily,
You being no longer here to remind me of your shortcomings.
Your pedestal keeps getting higher, as, busy troweler,
I add to it stone by stone.
But you could never bring yourself to apologize,
Until it was too late and I was too far gone to accept it.

And you never could understand why the word "divorce"
Came so readily to my lips.
For you love was all-in and forever no matter what,
Whether you were a bitch sometimes or not,
While mine was all conditional,
Not accepting our constant falters and failures,
Lapsing into those causeless insane contests,
Every one an evidence to me that no progress was being made,
Could ever be made.
Just hand me the towel so I can throw it in.

And as if blindly acting out
Some genetically programmed curse,
I left you when M was only two,
Just as my father had left me at that same age,
Never to return.
In his case, that is.
In our fairy tale the curse was actually broken,
I returned, and stayed the course,
A course so much smoother after I especially, but you too
Gave up the drink.

Always growing smoother,
Year after year,
But never smooth,
Because 25,000 quills a porcupine has.

3

72ND & AMSTERDAM

Still I see you. So many visions of you. Flashes. As if too much to bear too long. I see you both near and far. But more far now than near. Surely you are not fading away from me.

You standing on the corner of 72nd & Amsterdam, waiting there for me. As I emerge from the subway. Coming from work to meet you. New York, our second home, I working during the day while you lonely roamed the streets and parks, sacrificing the daily comfort of your home town companions to voyage alongside of me. Braving alone the fun-house world of the New York streets—and down under them too—the subway—the filth, the crush, the anxiety about boarding the wrong train or alighting at the wrong stop, looking away from the rats snuffling for food down on the tracks, the waiting for a train you are not sure will ever come, or when it comes will be the wrong one because you have become lost and confused in the underground maze—the propositioners, the gropers, the desperate disturbed of every sort.

So much waiting for me over the years. Many times right there, at 72nd & Amsterdam. That last time, our annual wedding anniversary trip to New York, a Thursday or Friday before the weekend, our 41st on Monday. Another jaunt on the Upper West Side. Explorers of a sort. Passing through landscapes is how I remember us mostly. Miles and miles on hard city streets, soft country trails and steep mountain ones, down so many beaches, from Acapulco to Tofino. On skis, in a car, on a train, a plane, the little motorcycle we drunkenly crashed in the field that Saturday night in college, the hot air balloon I insanely let you talk me into near Jackson Hole, a kayak in the San Juans (the orcas are coming!), a motorboat in the Abacos, a ferry out of Vancouver, an express subway train zooming by intriguing stops that we vowed to go to next time, on various water-courses quarreling in the "divorce canoe."

But especially now, probably because of what happened "next," I see you, standing there, at 72nd & Amsterdam, so often, that exact scene, that view, imprinted. The last time I saw you there, late November, the northwest corner, at the edge of the scruffy little oasis there (some benches, trees, a newsstand, was there also a swatch of grass?) next to the station on that side of 72nd on the little island between Broadway and Amsterdam (just above where the two streets cross and switch sides west to east (how could that be?! confusing me for the longest time)), cater-corner from *Gray's Papaya*. I forgot what we did that night, but I have not forgotten seeing you there, 25 yards away, that surge of anticipation, so often felt (beginning 45 years before, you stepping down from the bus, visiting me in my college town), each time not unmixed, from almost the very beginning, with a foreboding—that we might falter yet again, losing track of the proper steps in the porcupine minuet, quills suddenly spreading, almost involuntarily (that remote cause), in militant array.

But it turned out there was something outside us to fear that night at 72nd & Amsterdam.

The cough . . .

CLL. Chronic Lymphocytic Leukemia. Harboring there, in you, for years. Cancer cells birthed in the bone marrow spilling into the blood stream.

It can be a very mild thing. The doctor told you that most people with CLL die of other causes.

But it was like sleeping with a venomous but languorous snake. If it stirs enough, takes sufficient interest, to lunge and bite . . .

I tried to ignore it of course. My way. Not denial but disregard. Until it really had to be faced. You reminded me bitterly once that you too were a "cancer survivor." And that surprised me. I never thought of it that way. But oh we speak too soon! Little trouble for several years. A couple of mild chemo doses. Even those scared me. I know you think it was just that I didn't want your hair to fall out, but I swear I knew, I knew the danger of that poisonous "cure."

And then the snake did bite, on that Mother's Day trip, you and M in New York. No symptoms at all at midnight but a precipitous terrifying crash, wracking chills and fever by early morning, as if wandering in an enchanted woodland you suddenly dropped into the foulest pit. Ambulance to St. Luke's Roosevelt, observed for several days. Diagnosis: Pneumonia, probably caused by the CLL.

You had never cared for your oncologist. No feeling in him, and you had to feel a person feeling in order to take comfort in them or from them. Barely recovered from the pneumonia, as soon as you could make it home, in emotional crisis, you changed oncologists.

And then it began, the series of errors . . .

The first doctor sent the wrong medical record to the new doctor. The new doctor read the record, at least presumably did, but failed to recognize that the patient sitting in front of her was not the patient described in the record. The first doctor's office had mistakenly sent the record of a woman enduring a severe leukemic episode that demanded immediate and radical medical intervention. That woman was not you. But the medical mind and machine leaped immediately into a very high gear, conjuring up an immediate hospitalization and radical chemo regime designed to conquer the galloping-out-of-control disease—*of another person*. And the really terrible thing, to me at least—the new doctor fairly quickly, before the chemo course began, did indeed discover that the record was wrong, but even after she realized the mistake and reviewed the correct record, your record, which showed no cause for such mad alarums, she still persisted with the chemo dosage prescribed for the dangerously ill woman in the original record now known to be false, not you at all.

I knew better. But I was suspect and cowed. I had always minimized the CLL. That came from a lot of places including simple unwillingness to face what was at best an unpleasant change in our lives and, at worst, doom foretold. I had always poor-mouthed the chemo, always taken audible comfort in the fact that "they say you will likely die of something else and in due time." You thought I devalued your victimhood ("you know, I'm a cancer survivor too"). Now the snake had risen and bitten, which made of me somewhat of a villain. "The Minimizer." So who was I to question and who would have listened and you would have resented me (thinking all I cared about was your hair not falling out) if I had said what I thought, which is "Why? Doctor, why in the world would you now, knowing she is not that person in the record with the rampaging white cells gobbling up the red, prescribe the very same massive chemo regime?" At bottom was it that gently talking doctor's fateful insistence on showing us, but mostly herself, that the original mistake really had not mattered, that this was the right thing to do after all?

Although possible side effects of the chemo regime were discussed, not once was the concept of "secondary malignancy" mentioned, which I only heard about much later and after it was too late. A second cancer caused by the cancer treatment itself. So, after a lifetime of holding a certain belief or attitude, and, sitting there, deeply troubled, at that conference table with the medical team, knowing about the snafu with the medical record, the misdiagnosis, the mismatched treatment regime that had been mistakenly devised and now was being inexplicably adhered to. And after a lifetime of speaking my mind, damn the consequences, especially to and about you . . . I held my tongue . . .

At first it looked like it was beyond wise of me to have kept my mouth shut. A week in the hospital for the first chemo round. You did not get very sick from it. You hair did not fall out. And, after another round of chemo, and some other chemical potions, "administered" (i.e. *pumped* into you) in an outpatient setting, the CLL, seemingly miraculously, was declared to be in remission.

Yet the medical records reflected a certain caution, a fly, so to speak, in the curative "ointment." A small nodule, thought to be scar tissue from the pneumonia, was detected in your right lung. The radiologists recommended a follow-up X-ray of the lung every three months.

Now enter the third doctor, a lovely caring man (who I am not sure I could bear to sue even if the evidence were irrefutable) now made his deadly contribution by X-raying you once in February, which showed no progression of the nodule and no cause for alarm, *and then never X-raying you again.*

So there, on that day in late November, you standing there 25 yards away, at 72nd & Amsterdam, waiting for me, I emerging from the subway, we thought you were cancer-free.

But there was that cough. Starting small but growing daily more vicious. Accompanied by occasional expectorations of small masses of bloody pulp. Clearly you wanted to tough it out until your next regular physician visit weeks away, but the cough was horrible, even I could not ignore it, and I insisted you go to the brand new urgent care clinic near our apartment. They wasted no time sending you to Roosevelt South for X-rays. The hospital sent the findings back to the urgent care clinic, and the doctor there called you in, telling you, with a look that told you even more than his words, "You need to see your oncologist as soon as you can," and I knew there would be no disregarding anymore.

On that very day we had been married for 41 years and together for 45. Always your favorite day of the year. I was scheduled to speak at a conference in New York that week, I arranged for a colleague to replace me, we hurried home.

Terrified as we were, fearing the worst as in our separate ways we both did, we could not know, really know and believe and admit, that your life was nearly over, and, most excruciating of all, that every minute of all the rest of it would be lived on death row. And we especially had not an inkling that *our* own life was over. For example, we never made love again. But that was only the most poignant expression of a deeper rift, the unbridgeable gulf, the boundless alienation, between the quick and the dead, animation and oblivion. I didn't recognize it until it was almost all over, but a wall came down, and we could do no more ever again but throw our voices over it. And we would not really ever, through that wall—*see* each other again.

Now I only have this recurring vision, you standing there at 72nd & Amsterdam, I walking toward you from the subway station. Despite the five months that would be left to us, we did not know, could not have known that, from the very beginning, we had missed our chance to say goodbye.

4

THE SECOND THEOLOGICAL VIRTUE

Distant lights that won't come closer
Garbled sounds from other rooms
Anguished prayers all unanswered
Sins repented but unforgiven
Delusions mocked by "Not" and "Never"
Wounds bandaged yet unhealed
Cries of love bring only echoes
Conjuring apparitions from phantom air
Hope is so much crueler than Despair.

5

CERTAIN PROCEEDINGS IN THE TRIBUNALS
OF A VANITY CALLED HOPE

In the courtroom of medicine the sentence was death,
Pronounced by an Asian doctor,
No outward emotion, speaking obscurely,
Spilling tragic beans,
But only after my oh so delicate cross examination.
After all, you were right there in the room,
Your fate being foretold
In quiz show format.
Is that what he said? Really?
Six to nine months? Until October max?
Unforgivable affectless messenger of death.
Luckily there was no gun there for you to shoot him with.

Why won't they just give it to you straight?
You have to know the code.
Stage IV.
What does that mean?
It has jumped from one lung to another?
Such a tiny leap. So what? What did that mean?
The whole ballgame, that's what it means.
Once it jumps . . . Over.

We walk out as if we still had dignity.
Dodging the furtive eyes of the nurses.
They know, and they knew when we arrived there but gave no sign.
Our jaws tightened, our upper lips stiffened in grim resolve,
But our lower lips trembling,
Because all we really want
Is to rend our garments and cry to heaven.

Of course, as the condemned usually do, we filed our appeal,
A second opinion from the wizards in Houston,
Brewing smoking beakers of chemicals and false hope.
The gifts from these Magi included—
Gaping acidic sores in your mouth,
Flesh-dissolving bile in your throat,
Puking the little you could eat into our old popcorn bowl,
Your hair falling out
The pathetic wig you put on for my sake,
Until you could stand it no longer and shaved your head.

Most wizardly of all, the Pleural Effusion.
An accumulation of fluid in the lining of the lungs,
Building up and pressing away the little breath you had left.
They sent us home with plugs in your chest, a tube, some bottles.
Nothing coming out, what are we doing wrong?!
If there's nothing in there to drain, then why am I gasping for breath!?
Amateur efforts failing, into the hospital for a week or so.
Another kindly physician shilling out snake-oil optimism,
A placebo you still needed perhaps,
A necessary step in the punctilious minuet of cancer death.
I, having secretly given up, could only think, *It wasn't enough for them to kill you.*

Another byproduct they didn't bother to mention—
Chemically Induced Euphoria.
Thus the episode of the Golden Retriever you named Finn,
Assiduously sought, ecstatically found, bought dearly, brought home.
Later I found and could hardly bear to read
In the abortive little journal you kept for a few days,
"Found a puppy. Wrote an email. Waiting until a reasonable hour to call the number. Worried that
I have missed him as he sounds perfect for me and my new life—activate me!—walk with me—
have a buddy and every moment be with me! Cross fingers and hoping it is time and meant to <u>be</u>."

Wagging, lunging, licking, barking, pooping and pissing crazy puppy
A disorderly beast for an orderly woman
Who now, in her rapidly shrinking world, could hardly get out of bed.
And we were of no help, leaving you at home alone with him,

17

Thinking then that we had both room and time,
At least until October,
Didn't the Asian doctor promise us that?
Finn lasted a week and then you had to give him away to a friend.
Now his name was Delusion and Defeat.

Back in Houston the wizards mumbled,
Again in oracular utterance not easy to decode,
Not a word of consolation, you will recall,
Just moving us on.
"You have failed to respond to our dark arts,
Proceed to Clinical Trials on a lower floor."
To which we fled, a Friday workday waning,
Desperate not to let a time clock postpone the final reckoning
For that writ of certiorari so unlikely to be granted.
Ensnaring us in a tortuous weekend of hopeless hoping
Demanding, pleading, begging, writhing in supplication,
PLEASE!

And in those lower depths we stumbled upon, finally,
An inverted miracle,
A teller of truth,
A young woman doctor in that court of very last resort.
Describing the available Clinical Trials,
What we had always suspected,
An experiment beneficial perhaps
To someone else someday.
Was it something about us
Or was it the weekend pressing on her (TGIF!)
That finally moved her to blurt it out.
Directly to M, one daughter to another—
"If she were my mother, I would take her home and make her as comfortable as possible."
Appeal denied. The sentence confirmed and upheld.
Writ of certiorari refused, the Supreme Court is no longer in session.

We drove past Houston's gauntlet of dismal strip centers to the airport and flew home.
I still kept searching for some desperate surgical all-or-nothing throw of the dice,
I am a man of action after all.

("Work is where he hides" you once said.)
But "No more" you said.
Ich Habe Genug.
Bach used three words, you only two.
Quite efficient, no decoding required.
The next day I called Hospice—
Come and help us help her die.

6

INCIDENTS OF LIFE ON DEATH ROW

Your world grows smaller and smaller.
You used to walk for miles and miles,
Famous for it all over town,
But now you cannot even make it halfway down our block.
Then suddenly the kitchen is a far country,
Soon the family room a distant destination.
Then the bedroom itself too vast an expanse to navigate,
The four corners of the bed all the territory left to you.
And time shrinks too
As your world races faster and faster,
On the express train to Oblivion.

**

One of my colleagues asks,
"Can you guys at least go somewhere to relax?"
Well, we thought so . . .
We thought we could take some trips,
Didn't the one doctor say last December,
Just three months ago it was,
That you would likely last a year?
In January we planned for two weeks in the San Juans,
The house on Haro Strait
Just steps from the high rocks
Where the waves crash and break, and fade away,
Nothing left but flecks of foam on the breaking wave.
A good place for you to die, we thought,
Without coming right out and saying so.

At that house of pure romance,

Native grasses sprouting from the dirt roof,
"The Hay House," little G, age 5, named it,
Where we gave the kids the bedrooms,
Taking for ourselves
A tiny enclosed porch,
Glass all around,
Hardly larger than the bed we slept in,
Old fashioned double,
Keeping us close,
Just as you preferred.

The whales passing by,
Haro Strait their commuter lane,
Stopping often right there before us
To chase down and finish off a fish they had trapped,
Or just to frolic,
Putting on a private show for us.
Watching them as we sit,
Or stand if you could still stand,
There on the steps, or the grass below the steps,
Or if you could manage that now,
Out on the rocks themselves.
As in the old days, we might have the CB radio on,
Straining to hear the chatter of the whale-boat skippers.
Where might they be now?
Are they coming this way?
All of us keeping one eye out for them
Whatever else we were doing,
You more enthusiastically than any of us,
"Here they come!"
But it is only April and you can hardly get out of bed.

**

Soon after your diagnosis,
We go to Santa Monica,
Another place you loved.
You watch the couples on the boardwalk
And say "I wonder if they know how lucky they are."

And also you tell me how you now stand
Outside
Your own life,
Observing it from another place.
Both of us quiet for a long time,
Trying to fathom out there
In those Pacific fathoms deep
The perils you will endure
On this solo voyage
On which you have been haplessly impressed,
Leaving me behind,
Having failed to protect you from that fate,
Fecklessly waving from the shore.

**

Just after the hospice interview
You are sleeping on the couch
I scrunch myself in alongside and hold you.
Clumsily, foolishly, surely making things worse,
"There is so much you won't have to suffer."
"I know."

**

Until, like the princess bewitched,
You fell into that deep, near constant sleep,
So troubling to me, so haunting me still.
You watched old movies,
Because, as I see now, this was not
Just a distraction, but your way
Of affirming, in these last days,
Your own Romantic credo—
Rosalind and Cary, Katherine and Cary,
Spencer and Katherine, William and Myrna.
Nutty dialogue, witty conflict,
Strange bedfellows ultimately bedding happily,
Except our screenwriters, mischievous imps,
Kept maliciously doctoring the script,
And we actors adlibbing further,

Ended up playing more than we wanted
George and Martha than Nick and Nora

**

You are cross sometimes.
The living must seem like intruders
Noisy revelers, however respectful they try to be
Partying at your wake.
But so few complaints
"I can't sleep worth a damn"
(When all you seem to do is sleep).
And one day, distractedly,
In oh-by-the-way manner,
"This dying can be hectic."

**

Your sister finds you struggling
With the door to the patio,
Trying to go outside.
She rushes to help you.
Weakly, but as savagely as you could muster,
You push her away,
Then fall.
After a long moment,
She afraid to reach for you,
You look up—
"What do we do now?"

**

After the V's leave, I ask you
"Don't you want to see more of your friends?"
"Not really."
"Why not?"
"It's nice to see them
But then it's
Sayonara . . ."

23

**

Business as usual,
Still making my obsessive way in the world,
Now to little purpose,
But the hair of a corpse continues to grow for a time.
In a courtroom in Brooklyn my argument prevails.
Thank you, Judge, I must now get home to my dying wife.

**

Dan coming home,
On the plane,
Your life is over,
As my own
Moves on,
Unforgivably.
"Mama, why is that man crying?"

7

A TRIP TO THE UNDERWORLD

They promised us everything. Santa Claus, the Easter Bunny, Resurrection too. St. Paul's sales pitch to the Gentiles: All-inclusive, one low price—Christ, Eternal Life included, no extra charge. Act now or risk Hellfire. And Hell, in this Aquarian Age having been deftly excised from the theoexistential equation, the resulting all gain-no pain proposition must bathe believers in such bracing balm that they fearlessly, lovingly, with serenely smiling faces, skipping go obliviously to Oblivion. Such a madman's hubris. Well, no, that word, the progenitor of tragedy, dignifies undeservedly a much lower order of thing—a conceit, a braggadocio, a mere bluster—of usurped dominion. But not so for the rest of us, we of deficient imaginations, we who lack sufficient capital to fund the Pascalian Wager. We, unfortunately, know, or think we do, that human dominion is but a bloody cannibal coup d'état. That, at least in one sense, we are the lowest of the animals, the only one who knows it will die. More to the point—Stay Dead—Forever. Infinity is a long, long time. Some of us, well, I myself anyway, do try to "buck up" for that (because we must) but still harbor, and let rise to the surface sometimes, a sniveling cowardly envy of the believers.

They promised us! Planted that seed of immortality in our heads when, as children, we had no defense against it. The big bright package under the Tree marked "CANNOT OPEN UNTIL THE END." But, before The End, they took it back! No box, no shiny foil, no festive ribbon. Alone, facing a wall of Darkness. Blink, Goodbye, Over And Out, All The Way Out, Never To Return. Much Courage required to face that, without, well, let's call a spade a spade, existentially shitting your pants.

So now, I, better than many others, able to imagine the horror of that imminent extinguishment of your Self implacably confronting you (as you know, I once faced an at least somewhat similar thing, trapped and bound, waiting for that wilderness fire to crisp me whole). Yes, I, imagining the constant blow-to-the-solar-plexus, literally breath-taking Knowledge, in your case accompanied by a real physical near-asphyxiation of the lungs, and hypoxia of the brain too, you thus oxygen starved in every respect, I suspected that I was the very one that had brought the curse of nonbelief on you, deprived you of that succor, snatched away that gift.

There really *are* atheists in foxholes. Waiting in that wilderness for that fire to fry me crisp, lying there, looking up at the black lid of the sky (if there were stars, I did not notice them, only a jutting knobby branch or two of the thicket that held me fast), I even tried to throw the Pascalian Dice, tossed a wobbly prayer to Heaven that gained no trajectory at all, came plummeting right back down in my face like a shuttlecock in a windstorm. But I knew, and still know, that my stifled Cry to Heaven would have been a far different thing if I could have conjured up an actual belief that there was really Anyone There To Listen. And having been so instrumental in snatching it away from you as well, I wanted now to return that shiny gift under the tree back to you. I mean, who gave one damn now about "the Truth"?

So I conducted much research, plucking from the mass of dross the most relevant and persuasive scientific evidence ("just the facts Ma'am"), three or four videos supporting the possibility that there was, indeed, life after death, and then I made--for Christ's sake!--what amounted to an *appointment* with you that evening. Solemnly, ritualistically really, announcing my mission in obscure language, not fully revealing either method or motive.

I sitting up in bed, you propped up by and tucked into me, my legs apart, your tiny eggshell of head against my shoulder, your diminished wasting frame mostly only bones now against my chest and groin and legs. We watched. The white light of course, the whole near-death thing. Most interesting of all, to me at least, the amazing reincarnation story, the child in Australia, I think it was, with the memories unquestionably lodged within him of a British pilot killed in the war. Not just any pilot but one with a name, a story. All very hard to refute or explain.

Somewhere in the course of this special private viewing you disengaged, moved away from me, assuming your now usual pose, on your side, your back to me. You seemed to be sleeping, but I wasn't sure so I kept the video going to the end.

And when it ended, I looked over at you, at your back, wondering if you had heard the rest, whether you were still awake, what, if anything, I should ask or say, and then I heard you, your back still to me, quietly and matter-of-factly but carrying the power of a thunderbolt to me—

"Did that make you feel better?"

And I knew instantly that you, my Eurydice, were gone, had gone to another order of place and things, one forever far away from me and the few inches of bedsheet that physically separated us.

In our manic anthill lives
We still, often without knowing what we do,
Blindly, like busy bees in bustling hives,
Re-enact the ancient myths, which even now remain so true,
But sometimes strangely skewed.
Orpheus did take up his lyre,
More desperate than brave, his love soaringly renewed,
Journeyed to Hell to bring her home through awful fire.
But it wasn't at all as handed down.
Actually he did not look back, did not
So ignominiously earn posterity's disapproving frown,
So foolishly squander his only chance to change her plot.
They didn't tell us this part so we didn't know,
In actual fact Eurydice
Refused to go.

8

UNDER THE REDBUD TREE

It is still the Age of Miracles,
You made it out of bed today.

We sat on the patio beneath the redbud tree you planted long ago,
Your handiwork all around us.
Red, the color of power and martyrdom, yours.
Purple, the color of penitence and mourning, mine.
Green, the color of renewal,
For someone else than you or I.
Right above us the sheltering limbs of the rapidly spreading redbud,
Grown far beyond what we ever expected it could.
Beyond that the gray roof, the budding oaks.
Above that, thrusting above the roofline,
The grand fir tree in the front yard,
Said to be the tallest such tree in our State.

We made a life here,
Surely to your amazement as well as to mine.
26 years in this house.
There was a time that we did not seem to be cut out
For creating lasting, firmly rooted things,
This garden, this house, this marriage.
It was you that held onto us so fast and firm
When I so often wanted to give up.
Without the fierce mortar of your will,
This house you will soon leave behind
Will surely come tumbling down.
This house already haunted,
I its living ghost,

No more equipped now to live with comfort in the world
Than 45 years ago when you took me in,
Like a kindly person taking a shine to a stray dog,
Of no particular breeding or looks or even cuteness,
Even the occasional biter of the hand that feeds him.
Then one of our moments——
"The door is open," you said, not opening your eyes.
I looked up toward it.
"It's not" I said.
"It *is*," you said, typically brooking no dispute, "the flies will get in."

Even now it was hard for me to let this pass.
But I did, thinking, but only silently for once,
Often wrong but never in doubt.
This was you, this was I, all of our lives,
"Never give an inch."
Until it was too late,
Until the inch became a mile
Of broken glass to crawl back over,
But, in letting it pass, peace was restored,
A simple lesson learned too late.
Was there anything but this, you there, in your last days
That would have stayed my hand, held my tongue?

So you lay, and I sat, there under the redbud
In that softest near-perfect 77-degree day in that cruel spring,
Marred only by a wind that was a bit too strong but soothingly cool.
I reading newspapers, drinking coffee, eating a Fig Newton or two,
Watching you die,
A bystander guilty somehow,
Tarnished witness to a mundane and wholly private atrocity.
Hard breaths, sometimes turning to gasps,
Lunging from your chest,
Vicious coughing
Whenever you tried to say more than a word or two.
In your old tie-dyed pajamas,
Nubby head, like a Holocaust victim,
From the chemo that had done nothing but devastate you.

29

We will bury you soon.
In that small graveyard, thankfully so close to our home
Where you so recently bought our plots.
Just in time, so to speak.

9

BRIAR ROSE

It was the last Saturday of your life.

I came upon you in the bedroom, struggling toward the bathroom. Staggering, now forward, now back.

"Can I help?"

"No," your head shaking back and forth so fiercely it nearly knocked you down.

I let you go in by yourself, playing as well as I could my pathetic role in that pathetic struggle for dignity I was helplessly witnessing. But you were in there so long, eventually I had to check on you. Cracking open the door the tiniest bit, apologizing as I did, I saw that you had once again ripped off the small pads your friends had taped to the edges of the sink and the cabinets so you would not bump into them and hurt yourself.

Let's admit, there was no love left in that look you gave me, only anger and defiance, a misery of the spirit, unalloyed and pitiless, a look that begged only for privacy and deliverance. Oh what vengeful fairy had your existence so offended?

I closed the door. Somehow you made it back out and into bed without help. You closed your eyes and fell into that trance-like state between sleep and waking that had become your ebbing life. I stood there sobbing. You paid no attention to me.

Here she lies. Briar Rose. There, so close but so very far, the distance between the quick and the dead—hardly visible beyond an impenetrable brambled thicket of razor-edged thorns and cactus vines. She left us one day when we weren't quite looking, weren't quite paying attention enough, stupidly unaware that forever was not something a year from now or even two weeks from now, forever was here, right now, and then it, and she, were both past us—forever.

Is this what "making her comfortable" means? May the words "good death" turn to ashes in their mouths. Does dying at home mean you are badly cared for by a husband who had no idea how to?

And then it came to me. How to chop through that thicket of thorns to free you. Later that evening, I called Hospice and said I wanted a nurse at least part time if not full, and I suggested a catheter. They put the catheter in the next day, Sunday, along with the machine to help you breathe that you had steadfastly refused due to "the noise." You were dead by Tuesday. I am sure the catheter and the breathing machine helped you to your death. I am also sure they made your dying much easier. You no longer needed to struggle, with all that was left to you, to keep from fouling the bed and soiling our last memories of you, no longer needed to cling so madly and desperately to that last shred of what made you who you were.

10

WORD AND FLESH

On the bed alone together that inescapably final time,
Your last Station of the Cross.
For us this bed, so many beds before, none after.
Mine the only living matter in the room,
Waiting for them to come and plug and zip and bag you up.
I lifted you to me and tried to hold you fast.
Nothing.
You were Nothing now.
I let you down gently though it did not matter.
I was never in an emptier room.
Nothing.
The brutal severing blade,
Cleaving Soul from Body,
Word and Flesh
Un-made.

11

LAST WORDS

A voicemail you left me a few days before you died:

"Hey, I love you.
I had the best day of my whole life . . .
Wracking cough for many seconds
on the patio all day . . .
Coughing
I'm so happy . . .
Even deeper cough and for many seconds . . .
I love you very much."

Your last words.
I have saved the voicemail.
I return to it again and again and again.
So happy? The best day of your life?
How could that possibly be?
Just merciful ravings of your hypoxic brain
Or something of another order altogether?

And as I listen, I vividly recall,
Long ago on a hasty business trip to London and then to Budapest,
I ducked over to Ireland for a long weekend,
Renting a car in Dublin, I drove the entire width of that tiny nation,
In the inevitable rain, through the spiritless little towns,
To the west—
County Sligo,
Drumcliffe Churchyard,
Under Ben Bulben,
Yeats's Grave.
On the gravestone this—

"Cast a cold Eye,
On Life, on Death.
Horseman, pass by."

Now, bookended by another tombstone, yours
I, reluctant rider, still at pause, not having passed,
Keep wondering if your cool eye
Surely unknowing even who Yeats was,
Revealed the truth of it to me.
I keep listening and listening and listening
But do not see.

12

RESURRECTION DAY

At your tomb
I sit watching
Though I know you will not rise
On this or any other Easter Sunday.

It is 59 and ½ steps from the graveyard gate to your gravestone.
The cemetery is tiny and sparse of tombstones,
Most quite old, some flat on the ground and covered over with grass, others tilted askew.
We had ground roses planted.
I bring potted flowers from the grocery store every week or two.
Most die soon, that's just fine, granting me small missions, reasons to return.

In summer, bunnies, bees, wasps, and butterflies visit too.
Your friends also come by often enough,
Just as you would surely have done for them,
Contributing such things as colorful plastic bulbs in a pot
To brighten your tableau through the long gray winter.
There is a small blue child's bench,
Also a much larger bench
Of gray-greenish stone that our friends the B's insisted on paying for.
On good weather days I sit on that bench and read the papers or do some work.

On the tombstone our last name in large letters.
Below that your first and middle names plus dates of birth and death.
Next to yours my name, only one of the dates filled in for now.
Below, the same inscription I long ago put inside your wedding ring—
"The One Of Us."
I have removed my own wedding band,

Because death has parted us,
Sundering that bond and dissolving that vow.
But on my right ring finger I wear yet another band,
Your fingerprint embossed around the tiny endless circle.

At our home,
Still there,
After three years,
In our closet,
Purses and shoes, still somewhat carelessly stacked.
Not like you at all, that carelessness.
Crisp white blouses,
Silk ones too—black, navy, rose
That sometimes I press to my face,
Hoping your perfume is still faintly clinging there.
The red and white checked suit,
Faded jeans, T-Shirts plain and striped,
Cream-colored cowboy boots,
A brocaded vest of black and gold and forest green.
Belts, gloves, so many other things that now belong to no one.
The deep purple terrycloth running suit,
Soft as you once were,
Before you became a wraith and then a ghost,
Before you left all weight behind you.

By our bed,
Still there,
The book you were trying to read
Just before you slept and slept,
Did nothing but sleep.
The child-size cashmere cap
For your tiny, nubby chemo-head,
Shorn of your waves of auburn-tinged hair
That I used to clutch in my hand when I kissed you.
The black leather billfold where you neatly stored your bona fides,
Keeping them close to you even as you died,
As if someone would be coming to ask for your ID.

In the kitchen,
Still there,
Your very image,
As you sit now as you always sat,
On the high stool at your high desk by the window,
Imprinted on the air itself,
Like a fallen leaf pressed and traced upon a page.
I see you clear and whole and feel your presence there like a phantom limb.
Surely I am going mad.
Surely I want to go mad.

But it was none of those things that drove me here today,
To sit once again watching at your grave,
Your own Quasimodo,
Where I can do nothing useful,
Only worship and regret.
No, what drove me here
Was not even noticing
Your tennis shoes
Still sitting by the door into the house from the garage.
No, not that, it was, instead,
Tucked primly inside those shoes,
Those little half-socks tennis players sometimes wear,
Yours trimmed at the tops with a dainty row of alternating pink and green flowers
Where the flesh of your foot once met the bone of your ankle.

13

DE PROFUNDIS
(A SPARROW'S FALL)

And, so, what of your little death?
Just another sparrow's fall?
No, I deny that, and proclaim here,
In the face of implacable destiny,
That your death was all of our deaths,
Past, present, future,
All of our tragedy and comedy,
All of our absurd plight.
Passionate life,
Eternal death,
Fruit fly destiny.
It was Infinity, not Oblivion, that you deserved.
Your tiny particular swallowed,
Swallows
All,
All of it.

You are, you become, you are no more.
Flecks of foam on the breaking wave.
This is the mystery of our existence
And its absurdity, its tragedy, its comedy too.
But the deeper answer to the deeper mystery remains
Unvouchsafed to me
Unsolved, though I seek every day, every moment
That sparkling buried grail
The only purpose, I have thought, of existence to obtain,
Humbly, gently, no longer a demand,
For the answer,

An arrogance I left behind long ago.
Only a glimmer and I would depart.
Not gladly, not gladly ever,
But at a bit of peace,
Nunc Dimittis,
Knowing I achieved all my diminished capacity would provide.
And I do understand that it may, in fact, be
The most blindingly clear light
That I have been and ever shall be
Blind to.

Did I blind you too,
Over the course of all those skeptical years?
Why did you go before me?
How could that possibly be?
On your own death row, no chance of reprieve,
Did you in those last delirious days,
The cancer gnawing your hypoxic brain,
In delusion catch a ray,
That glimmer much prayed for,
But then left without telling me,
Left before I even knew you were leaving,
Harboring the secret,
Holding it tight to your breasts,
Under your bed cloak of deepest purple,
Wrapping you into Oblivion?

Like the priest of olden days,
Though now defrocked and unblessed,
I raise up and offer to all who consent to witness
The shining chalice of your sparrow life and death.
I loved you and I love you now.
At the end that's all I know.
And also this—
We are, we become, we are no more.

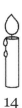

14

"I PAID THEM THE THINGS I NEVER TOOK"

When you looked down on me that morning, trying to disguise your impatience, and asked me when I was going to get up, I think I said, or if I didn't say it, I wanted to say it, if not to say it then *to look it at you,* "Dan, you don't seem to understand that things aren't quite the same anymore. I'm *dying* here." I think you understood my look. Your look told me that. "Crestfallen" might be the right word. Those beautiful grandchildren, G and F, reasons (along with you and M of course) for my being, they must think I am rejecting them. And I guess I am. I can't bear to leave them. I especially can't bear for them to see me this way. I can't bear them standing by this bed, trying to understand what has become of me. They don't want to be here. Nobody sane would want to be here. I don't want them feeling guilty or anyone making them feel guilty because they weren't solemn enough for the occasion.

I'm afraid more than anything else they won't remember me. What does it matter? It shouldn't, but it does. And I'm even more afraid that if they do remember me, they will only remember something they would rather not, a bald, wheezing, helpless thing chained to a fouled bed. Oh God I hope not, spare me that last thing. What does it matter? But it does.

So hard to talk to them, to anyone. This cough. So hard to think (and I do think it is spreading, I think my brain is sizzling with it). I don't know where I am sometimes. Just as well. I can tell, I think, that you wonder why I don't talk much. Well, the cough is a lot of it, but also I've said some things, and I've seen the look on your face, other people's faces. Best not to see those looks again.

Here, at the end, I am something I have never been before, all alone in my own cocoon, not a support but a burden to all. Did they do this to me? You said you will sue them if you find out they did. I really believed I had escaped the curse. That day when they told me the leukemia was gone. All the women on my mother's side. Except only herself, Mother, sitting in the home, body strong, mind gone. Saying, when she sees me, "Hi, M," and once even "Hi, Dan." But never "Hi, C." I can't help thinking that means something deep. I told you the timing was suspicious, that they "had to get married" because of me. She and Dad were so hard to love. I think you said, or something close to this, trying to console me, that I would not have to suffer that, maybe it wasn't *that,* the Alzheimer's, maybe you weren't so specific, but I'm sure that's one of the things you meant. It irritated me when you said it, but, I have been coming more around to it lately.

I hate to go, but desperately want to go, as fast as I can. Wanting it so much to be over but something in me still desperately holding on. I want to be brave, but I have to be brave all day long, and even all by myself in my own mind, and it is hard to be brave all day long and even in my own mind.

They say you can starve yourself to death. I'm trying to do that. Nothing tastes good anymore anyway. But I'm still hungry. Why am I still hungry?

Hanging on this way. I summon up some courage but then it fails me. For so long I hoped for a miracle. Why not? Though it just prolongs the agony really. That's gone now. Not that all of it is bad. There is the purple chaise by the window in the family room, where I can lie back and sleep and open my eyes once in awhile to look out at the patio and the garden. I always loved the sun. N won't let me go out sometimes, says it is too cold. I get mad at her, but she has been so good to me. Such a good sister she has turned out to be.

I'm afraid I won't, well I know I won't, ever laugh again. We used to laugh so much. Lately I've been so cross with people. Especially M. I so worry that she's not strong enough. We were too close, she and I. Selfish of me, I suppose. But not cross with you so much. I can't actually tell you for some reason, maybe I'm afraid you wouldn't take it the right way, but I forgive you. It was all worth it. Not this. This is worth nothing. I hope you can forgive me, I hope you have already, it was always so hard for you to forgive. "You're a hard man," I always said, and you were, and are, but deep inside, as I told you so many times, just a sad abandoned child, all of the rest of it a big thick tough scab over that first wound. That's why I could forgive a lot of the other in you. You were hard to love sometimes too. I as well. Both of us damaged goods from the start. Probably not that much different than anyone else. Who said, if we all put our troubles in a pile in the middle of a room and could choose from any of them, we'd take our own right back?

But I wish we had been kinder to each other. All that stupid fighting. But we still made a decent enough life despite everything. Adventure after adventure. You took me with you all the way. And I went too. Even though so often you didn't think I would. But I always knew I would, from the very first time I heard you spin out those dreams of yours. But you needed a compass and a brake, and that was me, and a Bitch too when I thought I needed to be (and maybe some other times too, I'll admit).

I hate it to end this way. I don't know how I thought it would end. Maybe both of us going together, next to each other in a plunging airplane. Or maybe as we were speeding down the road, your bad driving catching up with us at last, laughing at something, and we would look quickly at each other, a moment of panic not quite enough to erase our smiles, before the crash. Or just holding each other, sobbing, like we did that morning in bed after we were at the vet all night, deciding whether to put our dog C to sleep. I never felt closer to you than I felt that morning.

I so wish we could have made it to the Hay House. Sitting on the porch, fading away slowly, willing it to end, watching for the whales to come. Please go back there again and again. I know you will think of me there. Those mother orcas, their young ones trailing behind, that would have been such a nice thing to see again. But it all moved so fast. And I am so sick. You know how I always hated sickness. Yes, I was a bad nurse. And here I am, sick to death, just a burden. This cough! It seems like it's worth dying just to escape it. You always said how I talked so much. Very high required daily word count, you would say. But it's different now. I would like to talk, believe me I would like to say things profound and memorable, but it all seems so far away, a shore so rapidly receding, and the cough would rise right up, and I am afraid if I started talking, I would start sobbing instead and never stop. I'm sorry, but I don't think I will be saying goodbye.

15

STREPITUS: LIKE A FALLEN EMPIRE

How I detest the trotting out of hope,
The fake "moral of the story,"
False consolation,
Empty reasons to "go on,"
"Strength for the journey" and all that crap.

I don't fear Death anymore.
You took what made the next breath worth taking.

And yet—
There is an ancient rhythm in our bones,
Answering the muffled call of each new day,
Like a shaving to a magnet drawn,
Hoping,
In our deepest place,
Despite everything,
To stick and stay.

Like a fallen empire,
I will embrace
The tyranny of bordered space.

Like a conquered foe,
I will bow down,
Dashing my sword upon the ground.

I will ponder on coastlines now,
Where sea and land their obverse each befriend,
In glorious conjunction both meet and end.

Yes, may we take solace in the certainty of our defeat,
We gave it almost all that it was due,
We were braver than we knew.

QUANTA [A BRIEF GUIDE TO QUANTUM THEORY (AND EXPOSURE OF THE ABSURDITY THEREOF, PERHAPS)]

(For G, From "Shirley")

Surely I am not just a variable in an
Equation
Surely there is more to this I than mere
Probability
Surely I am not entirely invisible until I take the
Leap
Surely I do not fail to exist at all until I collide with
You
Surely not just a dead-stiff cat in Schrodinger's box until
You
Lift
The
Lid.
Meow!

LINCOLN BLVD., HIGHWAY 1, LOS ANGELES

Who says nobody walks in L.A.?

The Latinos are on the move,
Gardeners, nannies, and maids,
Gathering at the bus stops
Roofers, hoddies, laboring men of every kind,
Searching out the next job, meal, sleeping place.
Or just illegal seekers on the make.
But these people never seem to be homeless.
Always marching as if they have somewhere to go.
El future es en espanol.

On the other hand the leisure class.
Spend their day not working at anything.
Except surviving until the morning.
Streaming up and down Lincoln Blvd.
Like the wild holy men on the dusty roads of old Russia.

Ancient ones on canes or walking sticks.

A woman pushing an empty wheelchair.

Old black man wearing huge earphones.

Another covered head to toe with soot and dust.

Limping man, gaunt, bald, guiding a guide dog,
Sits down on the curb to read
Catcher In the Rye

That woman there on the bus stop bench,
Eyes closed, rocking back and forth,
Holding a small dog like a baby on her shoulder,
Burping him.

Young Amazon strolling along the sidewalk in front of the Starbucks,
One bag over her shoulder, another in her left hand, big stick in her right
Singing, vigorous and loud, concert-hall style.
Sometimes brandishing that shillelagh,
Waving it like a conductor's baton, conducting herself.

Black man,
Jean shorts to knees
Where they meet his long black socks,
Chattering at anyone who makes the mistake of catching his eye.
His back-pack seems to be fashioned from, yes,
A milk carton!

And here, a few minutes later, the survivalist.
Mohawk, fatigues, combat boots shined bright
Old-fashioned metal framed pack
Jerry-rigged from a small metal chair!

Who says American ingenuity is dead?
Who says entrepreneurship is done for?
That nobody wants to work hard like in olden times?

Yet these untethered ones are not here for our amusement.
They might just shit in your yard or cut off your head.

But indeed some people do walk in L.A.

Rocks from the road, hurtling up from the churning tires, banged at the bottom and sides of the car. The drive to the trailhead was much farther than he had anticipated, past miles of scrubby second growth forests, purple wildflowers sprouting chaotically among the ruined stumps and improbable new trees. He wondered if he still knew how to change a flat and what they would do if he ran out of gas.

The little girl held her nose against the smoke of his cigarettes and kept asking when they were going to get there.

They stopped in a little logging town and bought cream cheese, wheat crackers, fruit, and soft drinks in aluminum cans.

She tried to get a station on the radio.

He wondered out loud if they were lost.

"Maybe we should go back" she said.

But at last they found the trailhead.

Logs and rough boards, hewn from trees along the way, many of them not more than six inches wide, were nailed together to make a soggy, slippery, labyrinthine boardwalk that meandered through the rainforest. They recited together the old nursery rhyme, "There was a crooked man who walked a crooked mile. He found a crooked sixpence against a crooked stile."

Building that trail must have been punishing work, in the rain, in the muck, in the half-light, a haze now yellow, now light green, the forest a miasma of brown and green and yellow, dripping, oozing, seeping, moss everywhere, white-stemmed toadstools with apple-red tops, ferns, plants that looked like rubber plants, plants that looked like seaweed as if the ocean had only recently receded from the dank land.

The only sound the dull roar of rushing water, ubiquitous and soothing. Thousands of tiny streams coursed through the watershed. As they made their way along the boardwalk, water moved under them, all around them. There were little waterfalls all along the trail, many of them concealed beneath the vegetation.

He heard the outraged caw of a crow. Otherwise he could detect no sign of animal or even insect life. No birds, no squirrels, not even a bug.

They stopped to read a sign along the trail. People had once tried to live in this place. A tiny colony of Danes. But the settlement had failed. What fools, he thought, to conceive the notion that they could really have made a life worth living here. To the west a trackless ocean, in every other direction an empty continent. His mind and heart reached out to them, over the long years, down through the dense foliage that had covered every trace of them, feeling with their daily trudging hopelessness, in the dripping forest, in the yellow-green haze, under the slate-colored sky.

"Dad?"

"Yes."

"What's the conversation?"

"What's that mean?"

"What are we going to talk about?"

"I don't know. What do you want to talk about?"

"Are there bears here?"

"I don't think so. But there will be lots of them in Alaska."

"Can I pet them?"

They talked about the wonders and dangers of bears until the trail ended at San Josef Bay on the Pacific Ocean.

They sat on a fallen tree on the gray sand beach and ate their cream cheese and wheat crackers and fruit and drank their soft drinks.

"Is that oil in the sand?"

"I don't know. It looks like it, doesn't it?"

She looked out across the water.

"What's out there?"

He followed her gaze out into the foggy obscurity. It seemed as if they were standing at some final outpost.

"I'm not sure. Thousands of miles of water, then Russia, or maybe China."

The gulls scattered at their approach as they walked along the beach. The ocean tugged gently at their feet, trying to reclaim them.

"Dad?"

"What?"

"How does the seaweed get there?"

"The tide washes it onto the shore."

"No. How does it get into the sea?"

"I don't really know."

She finished drinking her soft drink and waved the empty can at him. "What should I do with this?"

"Drain it out and put it in my pack."

He did not unshoulder the pack but squatted down on his haunches so she could go behind him, open the pack, and deposit the can. When he stood up, he lost his balance and nearly fell over; a tiny sinew snapped in his back.

"I'm getting old."

"No you're not. When you're 80 or 90 you're getting old."

"When you're 80 or 90 you're about dead."

"Gramma is 90."

"Great Gramma. She's 92. I don't know if I want to live that long."

"Me neither. I guess. Why not?"

"Don't want to be dependent."

"What's dependent mean?"

"Other people having to take care of you."

"You take care of me."

"That's different."

"How?"

"I don't know. It just is. You're little. You're supposed to be taken care of."

"When I die, will I be born again?"

"Some people believe that. The Hindus. Other people believe you go to heaven."

"And kick an angel. And go to hell and kick the devil."

He laughed. "Where did you hear that?"

"Nowhere."

"Then there are some people...like me...who believe that when you die, that's it. Nothing. Lights out. Like sleeping forever. But no dreams."

She walked on, looking down at her tennis shoes, a miniature of him, the same facial features in a smoother, softer female version.

"Nobody knows. They believe different things, but nobody can prove anything."

"Why not?"

"Nobody's lived to tell."

"When I was little, I used to think you went to heaven and had a life."

"You're not so big now. You're only 7."

"I mean when I was 4 or 5."

"You mean a life like you have here?"

"Yes, except with angel's wings. Nobody told me that. I just believed that."

"How did you know what an angel was?"

"I don't know."

"Do you know what 'believe' means?"

"No."

"Believe means you accept something as true even though you can't prove it's true. Like God. Nobody can prove He exists."

"But He lives in people's hearts, doesn't He?"

"Well...I guess so."

Again they passed the sign that told of the failed Danish settlement. What could they have been thinking? They had tried to build a life in this drizzling place, here at one of the fringes of the world, isolated from all other human connection. Walking back along the trail he felt strange, almost dizzy, a kind of vertigo, as if he were about to merge with the forest but not knowing where to enter, suspended in an anxious agony of apartness.

She skipped along ten yards ahead of him, hopping from tree stump to tree stump, hatless, her blonde head bobbing along erratically, her lime green slicker shining against the duller greens and browns of the forest.

He caught up with her. She had stopped to examine a dead tree that had fallen across the trail, covered with the thickest mat of moss he had ever seen. Out of the moss grew a young tree, already eight feet high.

"Where do the little trees come from?"

"From seeds."

"Where do seeds come from?"

"The tree grows, and seeds grow inside it, and at a certain time of the year the wind blows, and the seeds fly off, and they land in the ground, and some of them grow into trees."

"But where does the tree come from?"

"I told you . . .".

"No! I mean the tree that gives off the seeds. Where does it come from?"

He thought, "The seed of the plant is its redemption..." He had read that somewhere. Long ago. He could not remember where.

She was waiting for his answer.

"Well...I guess that gets us back to God" he said, mumbling, uncertain.

"What I don't understand is what about God's father and mother?"

"God doesn't have a father and mother. We're created. He is uncreated. He was always alive.

"He's still alive," correcting him, as if uttering an obviously manifest truth.

"He's infinite."

"What's infinite mean?"

'It means forever. Not born. Will never die. No beginning. No end. That's what some people believe anyway. But nobody knows."

"Well, maybe God's not a person. Maybe He's an animal. Maybe He's a cloud. Maybe He's a tree."

She skipped ahead of him.

Along the trail two giant trees had grown up separate for a time, then joined each other and now grew together, self-made Siamese twins, as if they had exercised a choice. Roots crossed and crisscrossed the trail, intertwined, a sinuous tangled maze, perhaps impossible now to trace the roots to their sources, as if all the separate growths of the forests had knotted together right there in that place.

"Dad?"

He said nothing.

"What's the conversation?"

He did not answer. She turned around.

"What's wrong Dad?"

"Nothing. Everything's fine."

She waited for him. She held out her hand, which he accepted without a word, without a break in his stride as he looked out somewhere, off into the forest. He held her hand all the way back to the car.

THE IRISH IN AMERICA:
AUNT KATE

My Nana used to take me to visit Aunt Kate every Christmas.
She must have been somebody's sister,
But I never knew why we called her "Aunt."
She lived in a little apartment with Uncle Harry,
But I never knew whether he was her husband or her brother.
He had a wooden leg.
She with arthritis most vicious,
Her hands gnarled nobs of pain.
Worked hard, saved up her money, made pilgrimage to Lourdes.
Bestowed upon me one year
A tiny bottle, the precious water of Lourdes.
Nothing, including the Lourdes water, ever cured her,
Always pleasant though, through the thousand needles of constant pain.
Suffering saint that she surely was,
I imagine her tiny mangled claws and twisted frame
Crouched in her coffin,
Eagerly poised to spring forth,
Whole and new,
At the Second Coming.

THE IRISH IN AMERICA:
MARY AND HERB

Aunt Mary lay in bed, sick, day after day
Downstairs Uncle Herb,
Her husband, I finally figured out,
Also day after day
Sat there at the kitchen table,
Saying a word to nobody,
Playing solitaire,
In both cards and life.

THE IRISH IN AMERICA:
ANNIE D

Annie D
Used to go to the dance hall almost every Sunday,
Taking me along sometimes, your semi-orphaned grandson.
I would hang out on the balcony, drinking Cokes and eating peanuts,
Watching the old people chastely fox trot away their weekday blues.

You and my long-dead Grandpa were storekeepers once.
Petit bourgeois, with the faults of your class but the virtues too.
Lost your life savings on oil stocks in the Depression.
You took in boarders.
They would walk through the living room as we watched TV.
"Hello, Bernard."
"Hello, Mrs. D. Hello, Dan."
Then Bernard would climb up the slightly creaking stairs to his rooms.

You sold beauty products door to door.
You sold corsets to portly ladies.
They would come to your house for a fitting in your bedroom,
Two single beds with white bedspreads mimicking the lace of Kenmare,
Where you and I would lie at night,
Listening to a churlish talk show host on the old wooden radio.

Mary, Maggie, Delia, Kate, Annie, and lone brother John,
Raised up on a hardscrabble farm in northern Kansas,
Mother dead, you the youngest, your father's house slave,
Carrying the milk pail from the barn to the house,
Skimming the scrim of cow-hairs off the grayish liquid,
Cutting and plating and nearly retching
As you sat down before the old villain, knife and fork at ready,
A dish of salt pork, the fat jiggling like jello.

All of you fled that rural idyll.
Except brother John
Who lived there in scurvy poverty

Until a stroke struck him down.
You brought him to your home.
I still remember that gentle old man,
Clean too, once lodged in your spic and span world,
Sitting watching TV all day,
Spitting tobacco into a Hawaiian Punch can,
Who, the family story went, had told his village priest,
Vicar of God wagging his clerical finger,
Scolding apostate John in the public square,
For missing Sunday Mass,
"Father, if you put your hand on your ass,
And keep it there until I come to your church,
You'll never take it off."

Once per year, during Christmas vacation,
You would dress me up
And yourself too, always in a pillbox hat with a feather,
Matching your wool dress suit,
Drive us over to the far side of town
To visit the Flanigan side,
Kin to the father who had long ago abandoned me.
Clara, Vera, Lulu, Lorraine, and Rosemary.
Not a man in that house.

Annie, you did have your faults as wife and mother.
They told the story of Grandpa John,
Being caught just in time in the garage,
One end of a hose in the car's exhaust,
The other in his mouth,
Because you would not vouchsafe him
The meager pleasures of your bed.

Francie, your hero child,
Before he had a chance to fail,
Died, a sophomore in boarding school,
Of spinal meningitis.
They say he vomited out his backbone
Through his mouth.

You never let your daughter or your other son
Escape the quicksand memory of that beautiful boy,
Preserved in the amber perfection of an early death,
As his siblings drifted toward failure in everything they touched in life.

But what a Nana you were to me,
Your home a refuge of neatness, order, and measure,
Deliverance from another house
Of drunkenness, domestic violence, and despair.
Snatching the child support payments away from my feckless mother,
So I could attend that very same boarding school
Where Francie died but where I escaped to and out of--alive,
Where I could play basketball hour after hour,
And read, surely I did, every book in the little school library.
Deliverance from the loutish hostile stepfather,
The angry raucous mother,
Serial bride of drunks, pricks, and clowns.

THAT SUNDAY MORNING

Annus mirabilis,
16 years old,
Cruising down the street.
Was it the Road to Tarsus?
Two laughing girls
Come lilting out of those mighty front doors of St. Paul's,
A blonde and a brunette, Sara and Renée,
Swinging their shoulder-length hair,
Was this the salvation the old saint promised the Gentiles?
I knew one and soon would know the other
Renée the brunette would teach me E.E. Cummings and Bob Dylan,
Also how to pine with unrequited longing.
The blonde, Sara, you were the softest thing I ever laid on.
I pined for you too, also without requite.
They wrote you such a lousy part
In the vicious soap opera of high school and its dead-end epilogue.
That someone so beautiful could have chosen so badly
From the preening males arrayed before you
Makes Darwin a liar.
They told me you'd become a heroin whore.
Surely just another sniggering boy's locker room calumny,
But if it's true, could I have saved you?
Or would you have drowned me too?
And would you be happy or sad, or just not care at all
If you knew that I remember
Two laughing long-haired girls
Come lilting out of St. Paul's
On that brightest possible Sunday morning
When all of us knew we were saved.

Ancient filthy clochard on the subway stairs,
Climbed to the very last step he can achieve,
Only a few more to go,
But he seems at his rope's dead end,
Cannot lift his piss-stained pants leg to ascend
That single last step after so many.
Standing there, exhausted, clutching onto the rail
For as long as I could bear to watch him.
He not asking, not seeming even to expect
A single outreached hand,
As the crowd parts and flows around him.
Should I help?
Done that before, it doesn't work out so well,
Complications seem to ensue.
Forget it, move on, they are expecting you, you have a job to do.
After all, we wade through rivers of blood every day.

DIDO REVISITED

The lady lachrymose, like Dido revisited, sits in her bedchamber weeping.

Sitting there, in the overstuffed chair, in the master bedroom where there is no master, not even a hint of masculine presence anymore, all the shades drawn down but one, as she looks out into the winter twilight, the empty street as bleak as life itself.

Weeping. It seems like all her life has been weeping.

Her weeping had always disgusted him. She wondered if she would ever stop, could ever stop, if someday she actually wanted to. Sitting there, in her old terry bathrobe, the sound of the hot water splashing into the bathtub, her chest heaving, the legal papers clutched in her trembling right hand, her left hand gripping the armrest, pressing herself down into the chair, trying to become one with it, disappear into it, never having to rise again. She hurls the sheaf of papers across the room with a strength that surprises her. It bounces off the mirror of her makeup table and onto the floor, she screaming after it, "You bastard. You son of a bitch!"

It is just a few steps to the bath where she will for just a moment wince in pain, which will quickly turn to the warmest pleasure as she slides into the hot bathwater that will soon be swirling red.

You take the razor and in one quick, firm, decisive move slash across your left wrist. Go deep. And then somehow you even have the courage to gouge and slit open the right one too. And then you just drop your hands into the hot, so soothing water. And you close your eyes because you cannot bear the sight of blood, your blood especially, and you swoon, a giddy ecstatic feeling as your life oozes right out of you into the water.

She had thought long and hard about it, came right to the brink of it, but the bathwater was luke-warm now, and above all else there were the children to think of, who could not be abandoned, as he has abandoned all of them, and she could not bring herself to inflict the curse of a suicide on those who remained, even on him.

Long ago, slinking off the plane,
Hung-over, debauched, faithless, ashamed,
When the tiniest thing,
Bob of bouncing blond hair
Comes plunging, running at me fast,
Grabs me, hugs me around my legs,
Welcoming the constant prodigal home.
You were my beacon, my lighthouse,
A memory of decency,
Keeping me barely holding onto the world.
Now, thirty years gone by,
You now afflicted with the family curse,
And it is I who have had to welcome you home,
So many times, too many times.
But not as a five-year old could do,
Not with a plunging dash,
A delighted hug around your knees.
You saved my life, why can't I save yours?
Daughter you run like water through my hands.

Dan Flanigan is a novelist, poet, and playwright, as well as a practicing lawyer. His novel, <u>Mink Eyes</u>, is set in 1986 and explores the "greed is good" dynamic and the cultural tensions and gender complexities of that era. It is a modern hero's quest in mystery-detective form. In addition to developing a screenplay version of *Mink Eyes*, Dan has published <u>Dewdrops</u>, a collection of his shorter fiction. He has also written the full-length plays— *Secrets* (based on the life of Eleanor Marx) and *Moondog's Progress* (based on the life of Alan Freed).
For more information, please visit
www.DanFlaniganBooks.com

Made in the USA
Middletown, DE
11 March 2019